How to Trade
Advanced Breakouts and Breakdowns
in Bull and Bear Markets

By

Rashid Rehman

Table of Content

Introduction

Breakouts and breakdowns are one of the most popular patterns played by almost all traders. There is no doubt that this pattern has the most profit capability and can be found more frequently compared to other patterns. When I say more frequently, that means a bit more in quantity and hence challenging to identify the quality setups. Breakouts and Breakdowns inherit the danger of losing money due to false and failing patterns.

Stock trading is the game of odds, if a trader plays high probability setups with more odds in their favor, the results would be profitable, else the failing breakouts and breakdowns will eat the profits gained from other patterns.

To avoid false and failing breakouts/breakdowns I have explained eight (8) pattern boosters in this book, these important pattern boosters will help you differentiate between high probability best quality setups and poor quality, failing and trapping patterns.

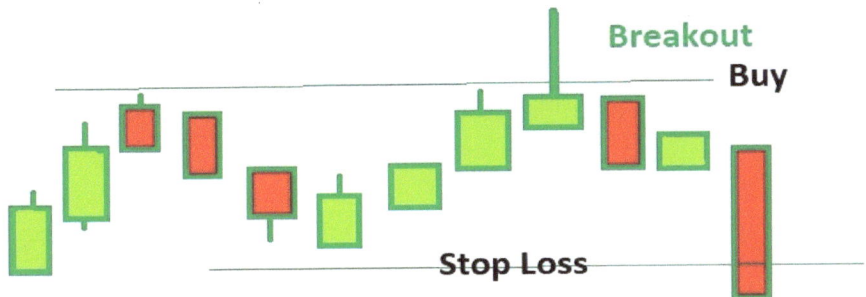

Once you learn to identify high quality setups, I will further explain in detail how to enter a trade, how to manage while in trade and obviously how to exit with maximum profits. This book will take your trading and investment to a very advance level, where you will learn how to write a trading strategy of a pattern, money management, share sizing etc.

Let this book empower you to become a profitable trader, the trader you dream about, a trader to say to their family and friends that I am finally profitable. This book is the key to many advanced concepts that will take your trading business to new horizons. Speak to you on the other side.

Intraday pattern and trading success

A stock can move in three direction at any given time. With that in mind there is a possibility of 33% winning rate when no strategy is utilised for trading i.e monkey style trading. That mean every trade executed with no trading strategy, will still wins 1 out of 3 trades, but the reality is totally different. It is possible that some traders execute trades with 3 out of 3 losing trades, not to worry, I was there once.

If we drill down to the contributory factors of traders failing that could be lack of understanding of basic math. Day or swing trading is the name of long–term game, losing less on a wrong trade and gaining way more on winning trades. The total sum of loses against wins in the long term should be a positive one. With positive results you will be considered a profitable trader.

To come out of losing streak and be a profitable trader, one needs to correct their basic understanding of math and probability. That said, the key is to only execute when a high probability opportunity present itself. Another important point is not to assume or create an opportunity and take a force trade out of frustration but to wait for an opportunity to present itself. Obviously, a high probability opportunity is a setup that meets certain requirements, which will be discussed in detail in later chapters.

How do I relate Intraday pattern to trading success?

As we have discussed earlier, the concept of basic math, an intraday pattern is the tool which helps us recognise high probable setups, with a defined low risk. In other words, to capture an uptrend on the higher time frame (e.g. daily chart) an intraday pattern is essential. In day to day life if we want to go to a place by public transport, we don't just jump on any bus. Every destination has its own bus with a route number, similarly a defined intraday pattern would be the bus that will provide safe, low risk transport to the desired target. For a professional and disciplined trader if there is no intraday setup/ Pattern they do not enter a position, by utilizing only high probability setup/patterns they increase their winning rate and hence overall profits.

Looking and scanning for a specific intraday pattern also help traders to avoid over trading, revenge trading and fear of missing out etc.

Doing the Right Things

There is no right or wrong in the world of trading and investment. Some people trade randomly as they think market movement is random, Other follows stricter criteria for stock selection and trade execution. The ''Doing the right things'' for a business is to follow a certain mindset at all the times to have a successful and lasting career. For a trader/ investor to be successful one should be clear on at least one of the following points.

The Concept of losses

The dictionary meaning for losses is ''the fact or process of losing something'', I am glad they are using the word process. Stock trading and investment is also a process from stock scanning to trade execution. Stock moves in three directions, I believe we know that. When stock moves in our favor we are said to be in profit, on the other hand when stock moves against an intended direction the result is a loss.

I am sure we have a lot of emotions attached to the term losses, but we should not forget that losses are part of the equation. All new traders have the urge to be right all the time with no losses but, that is not the case. Successful traders do not concentrate on losses as they keep their emotional balance in check and save that energy for the next opportunity.

Working in our best interest

With new traders and developing traders they often have issues around overtrading, revenge trading, fear of missing out or not taking a position. All these symptoms are not a good sign and must be identified and treated. So how to cope with those short comings could be a huge topic and may vary from individual to individual. To overcome the fore-mentioned issues I always remind myself '' am I acting in my best interest'' or I am working in someone else's interest. Markets are an emotionless machine, it does not take into account personnel circumstances or how hard you worked and saved capital for trading. To be successful, one should always act in their best interest by having a trading/investment Plan with all the strategies, risk amount, entry exit and in-trade management plus max day loss limit etc.

One of my great mentors, a professional trader once told me to keep your daily life clean of conflicts and negative emotions, so that those emotions do not influence your trading decisions. And the reality is, our brains limit its capability when our brains go through certain emotions. A good research on brain capability would be fight or flight mechanism, have a read on this topic, the Fight or flight mode can affect our ability to execute trades flawlessly. I can write a lot on relaxation etc but I want to keep it short and sweet, so a simple solution to get out of fight or flight mode is to meditate or sit with someone and have a laugh.

Importance of Goal Setting

We all need a compelling reason to keep us on track. In day/swing trading there are usually no one watching us, we take decisions based on our knowledge, belief etc. A proper goal should always be there to keep us motivated, to do the right things and work in our own best interest.

Track your Trades

If you want to be successful in this business, it is very important to record all your trades. You can record your trades by writing each trade entry, exit, the reason for entry, a reason for exit, Risk unit gain or loss and your feelings while in trade. By recording this data, you can go back and analyse your trades, you can find out what works and what not. Overall tracking and recording will help you identify your trading shortcomings and help improve the areas. Also, tracking will help identify the patterns you are good at and making all your money.

I bet you don't know this

What exactly is stock trading or investment. Stock trading is a game of decision making under the condition of uncertainty. The reason why we trade or invest in stocks is to make money but there is a factor which is limiting our ability to make more money. The limiting factor or the actual problem all traders are facing is **uncertainty**, if we somehow reduce the level of **uncertainty** the chances of trading in the right direction will increase. We can reduce uncertainty by finding high probability, high odds, clear and proven stock setups, once uncertainty is reduced and we execute trades flawlessly the outcome should increase, obviously the outcome in trading is profits (Money).

The other important aspect of reduce uncertainty is to make our decision process easier. As long as the trading decision is easier and simple, we can execute the trades with less emotions and more confidence and increase profitability.

Also, stock trading needs a bit of imagination, every time we see a setup halfway, we should be able to imagine all possible scenarios. That means with our mind eye we should see how the candles will look when the stocks go up and what would be the structure when the stocks failed to move in the intended direction.

In this strategy book we will discuss all possible breakout and breakdown scenario(s) which a stock can go through, this will reduce the uncertainty and make our decision making easy. I will also explain in detail how to manage different scenarios, which should help improve the psychology side of your trading.

Breakouts / Breakdowns Explained

Breakouts are the most known and discussed setups in stock trading world. Most of the old successful traders used different terminologies for this setup like, out of the box, going above the base, accumulation etc. When I started trading and started to read about breakouts and breakdowns, I thought I knew everything, believe me you won't find the actual valuable information for free. I must say you will learn something very new in this book about high probability breakouts and breakdowns.

I remember I used to trade cup and handle pattern, which would always fails when the handle try to go above the cup. It is true that the locations we were thought to buy are actually selling points for professional traders.

In professional trading, breakouts and breakdowns has some clear signs in term of candle formation, volume and location of the consolidation etc which we will discuss in detail. I will not finish this book till you know all about high probability breakouts and breakdowns.

How does the pattern look like?

An initial move up by a catalyst which is usually very hard to catch, followed by a moderate period of consolidation and a move above the consolidation. The consolidation is the interesting period which is seen by a lot of traders around the world and its important to note that not all consolidation are equal. We will discuss further in the strategy section what boosters to look for when hunting for breakouts.

Let's look at the mass psychology during the consolidation phase. The initial move up usually has some shorts covering their positions plus buying through open orders, also there is usually a hedge fund or bank beyond the initial move up supporting the stock. With the initial up move the party which bought the stock at lower price start selling. For every seller there should be a buyer, imagine a large hedge fund trying to partially sell their position, their partial position would be in millions normally. It

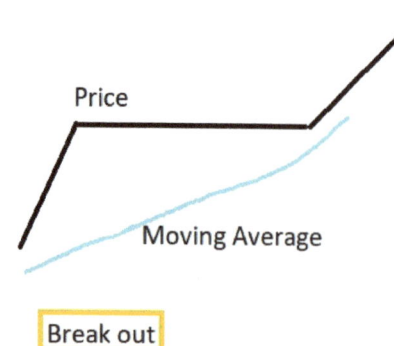

will take another big party to observe that amount of supply.

The selling of one party or parties and the buying of others creates the narrow range. As I mentioned earlier the parties could be market makers, hedge funds, banks, chat rooms and individuals. The price stays in the narrow range forming a tight consolidation base with a temporary breakdown of the base and return to the range again. The temporary breakdown also known as the false breakdown or a shakeout, will basically shakes out weak hands and the price will move back to the range. The shakeouts usually have high volume where the algos and other bid hunters buys the stocks.

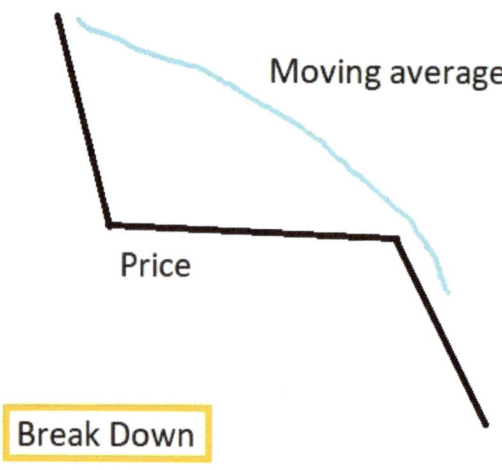

In another type of breakout the volume dies away and people think the stock is gone dead and a few weak hands get rid of their position. Overall a high probability breakout should have some type of trick which will shake the weak hands out. The weak hands usually chase the stock and buy again when the price moves up a few candles as they can't tolerate the up move.

Also, before breaking out to new highs the narrow range should have a very tight base where one can draw a horizontal line on top of the range. Finally, the range expands, and the price moves up to new highs. After the breakout, the groups who were short start covering their position and the professional traders start buying hence the price go higher. In the strategy part of this book I will explain where to buy and where to put the stop loss.

IF you are trading of the 5-minute charts, the price usually breaks out when the 20ema reaches the price or the price shake out and touch the 20ema. Remember that ema and sma are lagging indicators and may touch the candles after the price broke out, this will be covered in the strategy section. For those who don't know, ema is exponential moving average and sma is simple moving average, your trading platform should have an option for these indicators.

Late day breakout and breakdown

Late day breakouts and breakdowns have the same concept as early day or mid-day break outs with the difference that this breakout happens later during the market session. The reason for a late breakout could be an awaiting news, market makers getting rid of their position etc. Shakeouts and low volume is usually part of this pattern. BTW in all breakout and breakdown patterns, the colour of the candles do not matter as long as the price stays in a tight range.

Late day plays start breaking out when the 20ema reaches the price on 15min charts. The chart should have all other properties as 5min, the entry criteria will be discussed in detail in the strategy section.

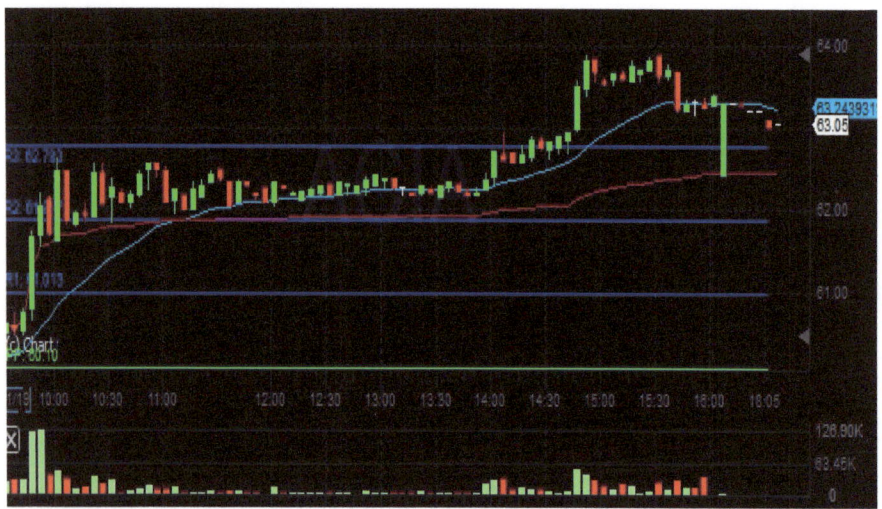

This is an example of late day breakout, look at the dead resting volume on this 5-minutes chart during the consolidation. The magenta color line is 20ema, the red line is VWAP. and other horizontal lines are pivot points that I use for other strategies, not used for breakouts or breakdowns.

The Pattern Boosters

Stock pattern booster is the most important topic missed from the free education available on YouTube, google etc. All my strategy books have explanations of the boosters associated with the patterns. Below is the explanation of the boosters used in this strategy.

Multiple time frame alignment:

Pro traders analyse stock on more than one time frame before entering a position, easier said then done but this one step will make you a consistent profitable trader. Taking a long position will require a clear up trending daily, good bullish daily charts are: level 1 gaps, daily breaking out of a few months of consolidation, breakout above a tight consolidation, in some cases price breaking above previous day highs etc. It's good to monitor and observe which daily charts moves more than others.

Relative Strength

Relative strength and weakness is a broad topic, shortly you should be trading in sych to broad market i.e symbols QQQ or SPY. If the market is bullish, all the long positions should work fine, while the shorts may struggle to go straight down. When the market is down the shorts would be fine to trade and longs will stay mostly sideways. In some cases, stocks are more stronger then markets e.g market gap down and stock gap up, even in this scenario we will follow our strategy and will not execute blind trades.

Shakeouts

Shakeouts are false breakdown or a false move in opposite direction of the intended move (see example charts). Once a shakeout occurs and price moves back to its original range, this action confirms that the buyers (in bullish condition) are in control and are committed to move the price up. Shakeouts comes in different forms, a move down and then up in smaller time frame could be a single bottoming tail in larger time frame.

Narrow range

A tight range with almost equal highs. Ideally you can put a ruler on top of the range and draw a horizontal line above the candles.

Half or Whole numbers

In stock trading half or whole number are considered significant as a lot of traders respect these numbers. The consolidation range should ideally be under a half or whole number. The trick is to buy above the consolidation in this case, as buying above the whole number usually mess the reward to risk, the price some time moves very fast and reduces the chances of getting filled. When you notice price consolidation near a half or whole number, keep an eye on that stock.

Same approach will apply to consolidation above half or whole numbers when the intended direction is down.

Major Support or Resistance area

The Price also consolidates below a major resistance or above a major support before breaking the area. When looking to play breakouts or breakdowns, support or resistance areas becomes an important booster for the pattern and make the plays more probable. In simple terms support is considered a demand area and resistance is a supply area.

Room to Move

That's one of the most important concepts used to judge the reward to risk of a trade. As a trader, we always make sure that a stock has no overhead resistance and there is enough room for the stocks to move in our intended direction. When shorting a stock, the stock should have enough room before it falls into previous support area.

Moving Average

I discussed moving average in the break out section, for a breakout trade the moving average should be raising, where as, for a breakdown trade the moving average should be falling. The idea angle of rise or fall of the moving average is 45 degree, which represent a smooth move up or down of the moving average.

The Strategy

You might know that I interact with a lot of traders on Social Media groups. I have noticed that even experienced traders call a candle stick pattern, a strategy. By now you should know that pattern is how price moves and which human emotions drive them. A price pattern without a strategy is like a powerful vehicle without fuel. A **strategy** defines what pattern or candle formation to look for, it must have boosters, entry management, in-trade management and exit management. Without any further delay, lets load our vehicle with the appropriate fuel and move on:

Time Frames to watch

I should say that professional traders get into a position when multiple time frame aligns i.e. to go long on a bullish daily chart, the pro traders will only enter a position once the lower time frame starts trending higher. To achieve multiple time frames alignment, professional traders watch time frames as mentioned below:

❖   From 09:30am to 10:00am (EST- New York time zone)
Time frames to watch are daily chart, 1min, 2min and 5min charts.

❖   At 10:00am (EST time) you should be watching Daily, 2min, 5min and 15min

❖   After 10:30am to market close you can watch Daily, 5min, 15min and 60min charts

Pattern Requirements

Must Have: A pattern to qualify for trade must meet the following criteria. Obviously, you can change these criteria to your requirements and understanding, the following is what I have found work perfectly.

1-   The Daily is a clearly bullish

2-   There is no immediate overhead resistance

3-   There is enough room to move (enough reward to risk)

4-   The stock is bullish on all time frames (MTFA)

5-   Tight narrow range bars consolidation (You can relax this with experience)

6-   A 45-degree rising 20ema (20 period moving average- ema or sma)

7-   Shakeout bar (this bar is some time a minor break down-engulfing bar)

Good to have:

The following items will increase the probability of the play:

1-   Relative strength with respect to market

2-   Half or whole numbers

3-   Significant resistance

You can write these requirements on a piece of paper and tick each as you look at the charts, once you see some or all the criteria in a chart you can plan to enter as per entry management. With time these points will in grind in your mind and you won't need to look at the checklist.

(The above criteria can be inverted for Breakdown plays)

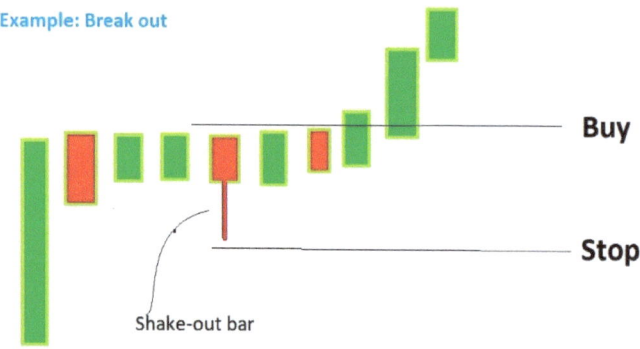

Example: Break out

Buy

Stop

Shake-out bar

Trade Management

Entry Management

Long Entry:

Once the ''**must have**'' requirements mentioned above are met, Buy above the narrow consolidation bars and place your stop below the shake-out bar.

Short Entry

Once the strategy requirements are met, Sell below the narrow consolidation bars and place your stop above the shake-out bar.

Remarks: Program Hot keys in your trading program to buy and sell, as accuracy and speed is very important in trading business.

In Trade Management

That's the tricky bit which no one talks about. Let me draw it, pardon my drawing:

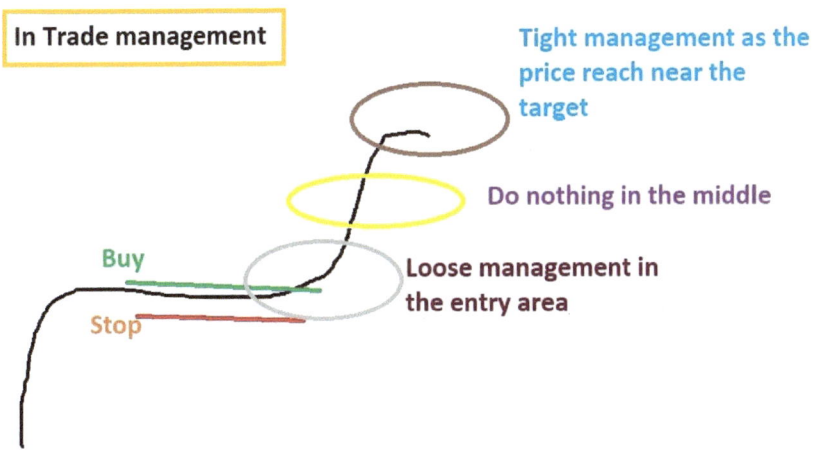

Entry Area:

Loose management is to let the trade play out. With experience you will know when to get out at this stage if you see any fault with the trade but for now let it play. It's better to develop all good habits to start with and alter the rule as you grow experience.

Middle Area:

Strictly do nothing when the price start moving in your direction. Let the trade enter the target zone. For your knowledge, the price sometimes pulls back to entry area, don't be shaken out by this as the price will move up quite fast.

Target Area:

When the price reaches the target area, we don't want to be giving back our profits, so the management is tight. A proven method of tight management is 1 min bar by bar. I will explain bar by bar management in the exit management.

(Hope you are enjoying this book; I have spent days and nights to complete this book. May I request you to leave a review for me on the main page.)

Exit Management

Let's dig into some interesting stuff

2R- AON:
2R-AON is two risk unit gain on all position or nothing, which means if you are risking $100 per trade you will exit all position when the profit reaches to $200 else you will take a stop loss.

AON:
All or nothing is an aggressive exit management strategy where the trader have a pre-determined target. The trader in this case is sure that price should moves to x point, so they wait till the price reaches that target point or take a stop loss. For example: buy near pivot point and sell All on R1/R2 or take a stop.

BBB:
BBB is Bar by Bar management, for example you entered a trade on a breakout using five minute chart, once the first 5 min bar completes and second bar starts, you move the stop under first bar(during the making of 1st bar the stop is under shakeout bar), once second bar completes and third bar starts you move the stop under second bar and so on, to the point when your stop taken out or target reached.

For management of the exit in the target area, switch to one minute chart and move the stop under every completed bar until the stop is taken out or the target is reached.

Moving Average:
Once your trade triggers you stay in the trade as long as the price remains above a moving average, you can use 8, 9 or 20ema for this type of management. Exit when price reaches target or closes below the moving average.

Combo management:
Trade can also be exited by combining some of the above exit managements. Eg one known way is to exit ¾ position once profit reached to 2R and manage the rest bar by bar, AON on the remaining shares or exit end of the day on the remain shares. (Obviously bring the stop to break even when you take a ¾ partial profit).

Share Sizing

- ❖ Share size is based on the risk amount (R) divided by stop loss:
- ❖ Share Size = Risk (in dollars) / Stop Loss

Example 1: Risk "R" per trade is $500 | Entry: $22.45 | Stop $21.95
- ❖ Stop Loss: $22.45 – $21.95 = $0.50
- ❖ Number of shares: $500 / $0.50 = 1,000 shares

Example 2: Risk "R" per trade is $50 | Entry: $22.45 | Stop $21.95
- ❖ Stop loss: $22.45 – $21.95 = $0.50
- ❖ Number of shares: $50 / $0.50 = 100 shares

Risk 'R' is the amount you risk per trade and the intentions on every trade is to make multiple of Risk amount. For example, if risk $500 per trade, your aim would be making $1000, $1500 or more per trade.

Suggestion: New starters should risk 30 to 50 dollars per trade to preserve their trading capital during learning and practicing phase. Increase the risk amount only when the stats prove that the trading results are consistently positive.

Note:

The reason we trade to a fixed risk because trading financial market carries risk, You can read more about risk on US Security and Exchange commission investor publication.

Example Charts

Following are the example of Breakouts, Breakdown, Late day breakouts and late day breakdowns. I use the following moving averages:

❖   **Daily Chart:** 20 sma, 50 sma and 200 sma (some charts have red 9 ema which I don't use any more)

❖   **1/2/5 min charts:** VWAP, 20 ema & 9 ema

❖   **15min charts:** 20 ema & VWAP

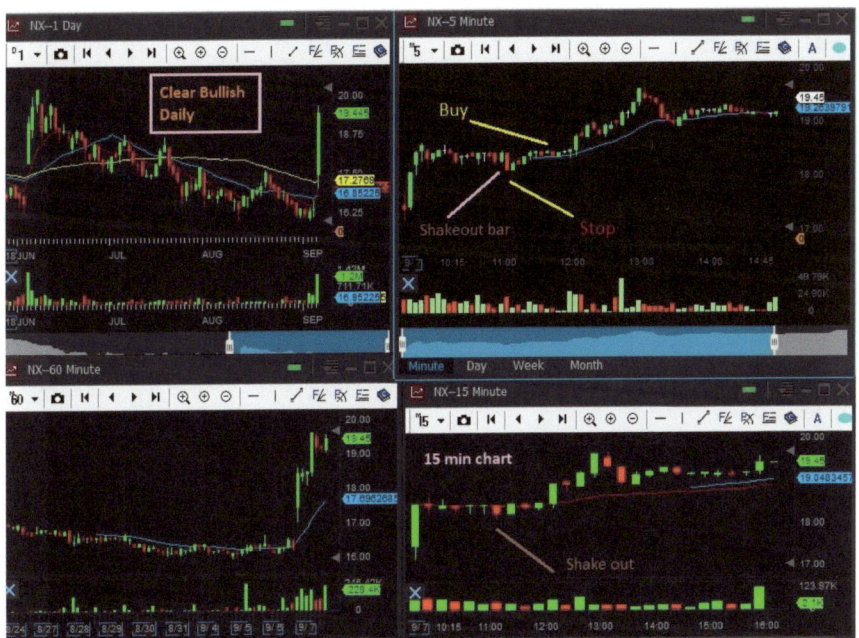

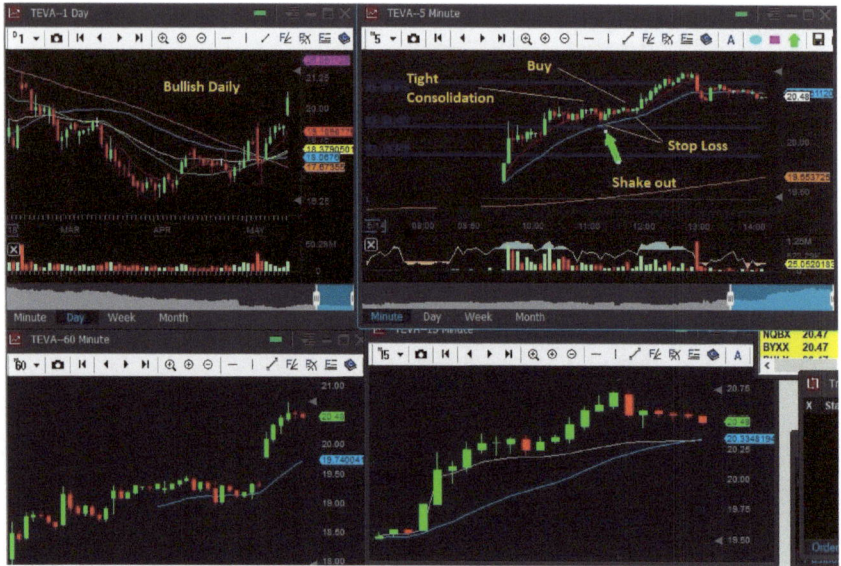

As I have mentioned earlier, the shakeout comes in different forms, Also the tight consolidation range may slightly vary in candle size and formation. With practice and screen time you will master all types of variations and will know these charts likethe tip of your fingers.

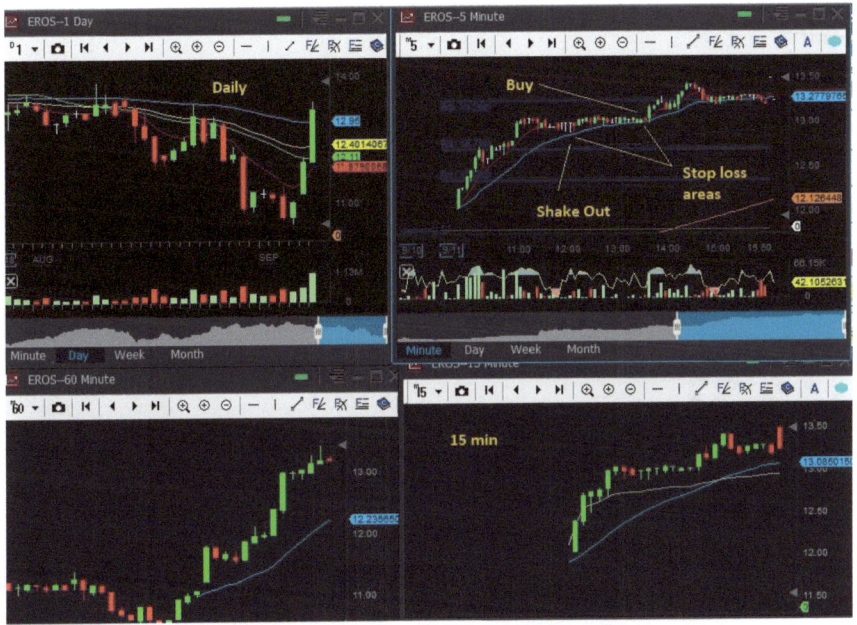

One of the benefit of breakouts and breakdown is tight stop loss, for example your risk per trade is $100, stop loss is 10 cents then the Share size for this trade should be 1000 share. In the above EROS chart, if we buy 1000 shares at 13.08, set the stop at 12.98, the stock goes to 13.45 that is a profit of 3.7R (3.7x100 = 370$ gain).

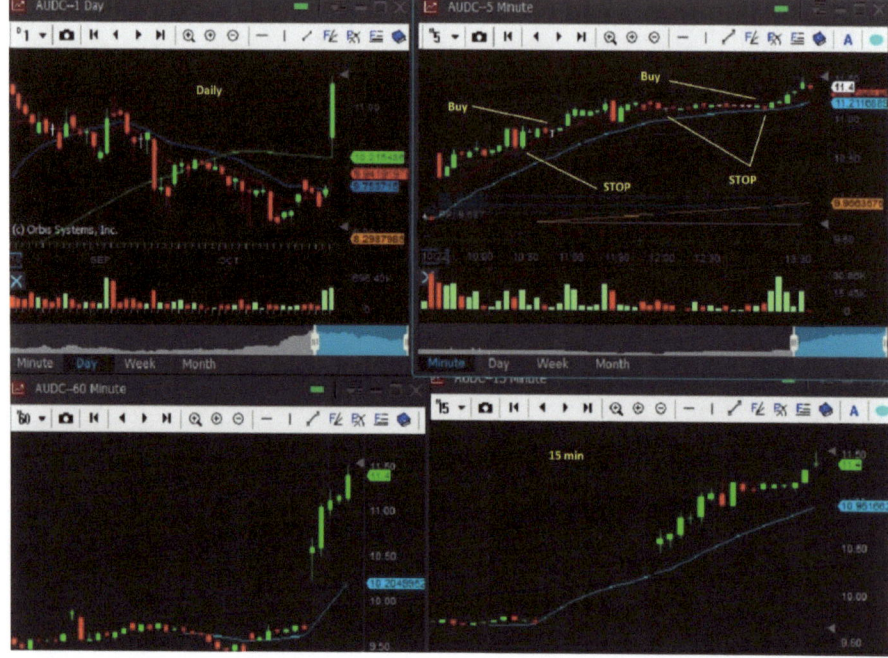

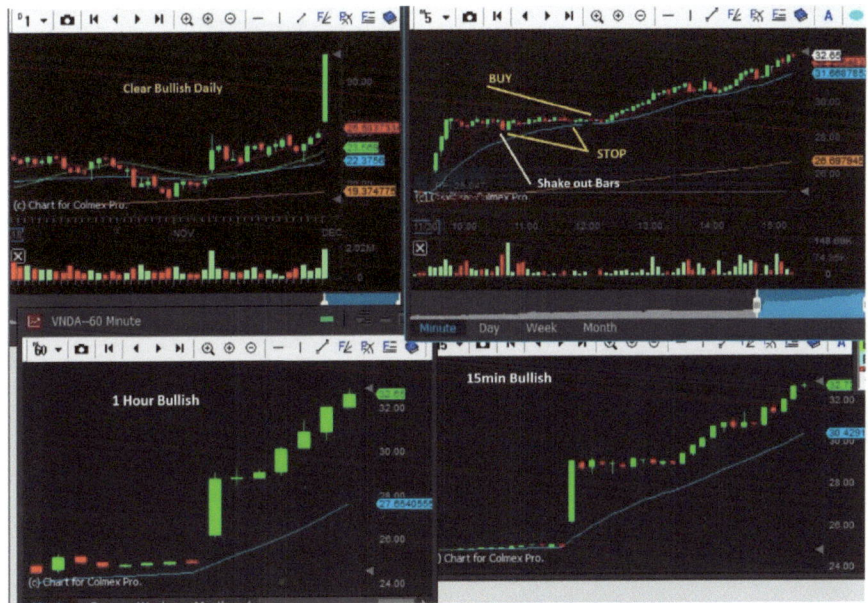

Multiple Time Fame Alignment- All time frames are Bullish

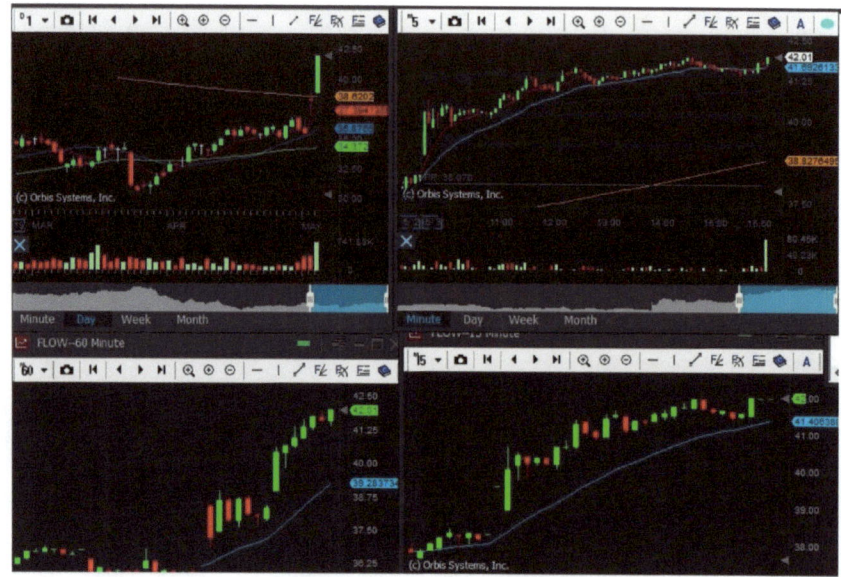

5 min Chart

Break Down Examples

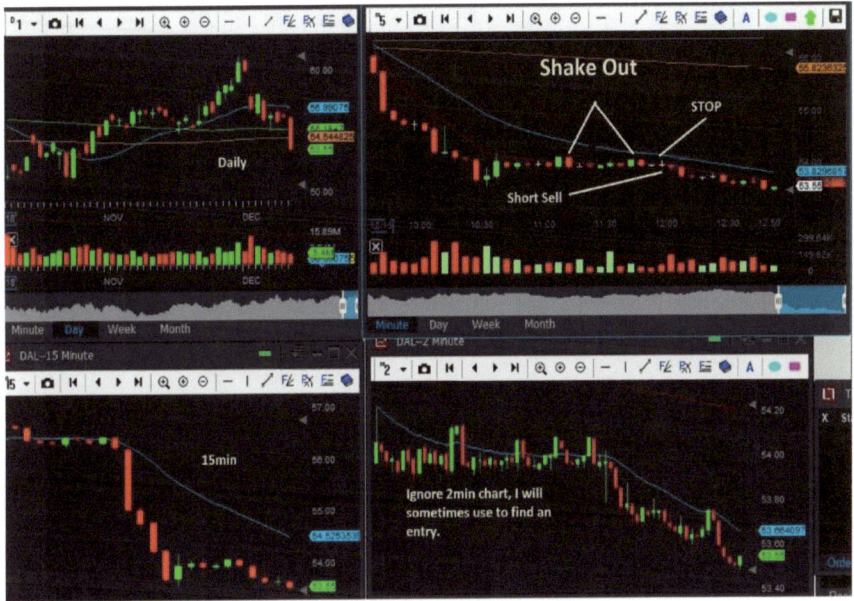

Note that the breakdowns are not different to the breakouts, we look for the same criteria i.e. compelling daily chart, lower time frame shakeouts, tight consolidation etc.

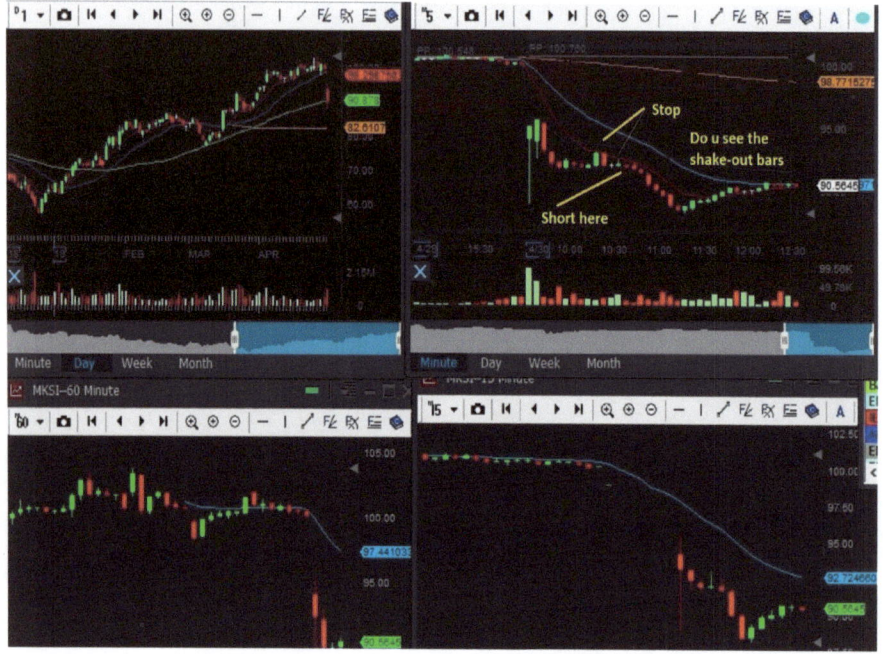

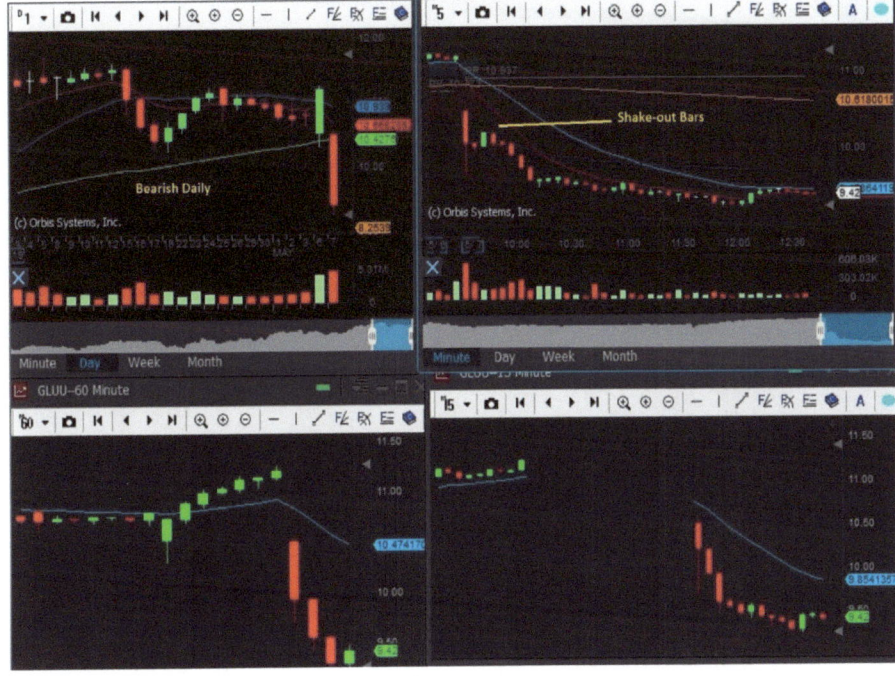

Late Day Breakouts and Break Downs

I love late day breakout and breakdowns. In the launch break I make a list of these charts and keep watching them for an entry.

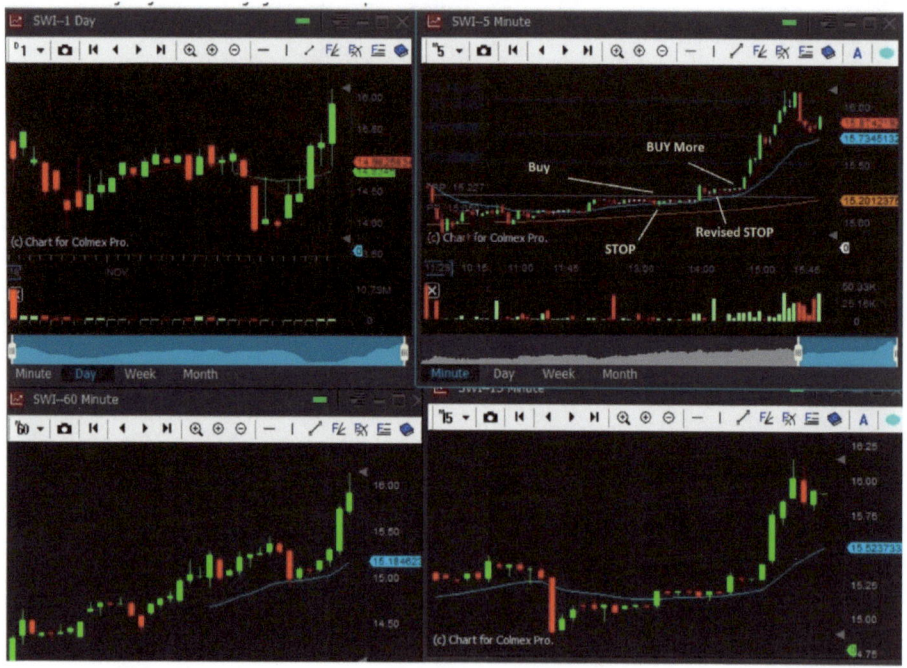

Imagine the share size where the stop is 3 to 5 cents, i.e. a low risk high profits trade

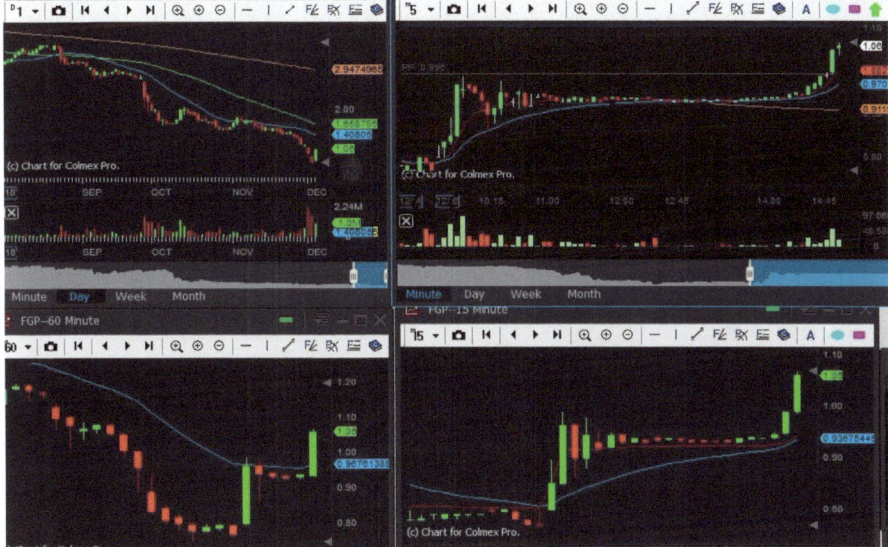

Example of late Day Break out

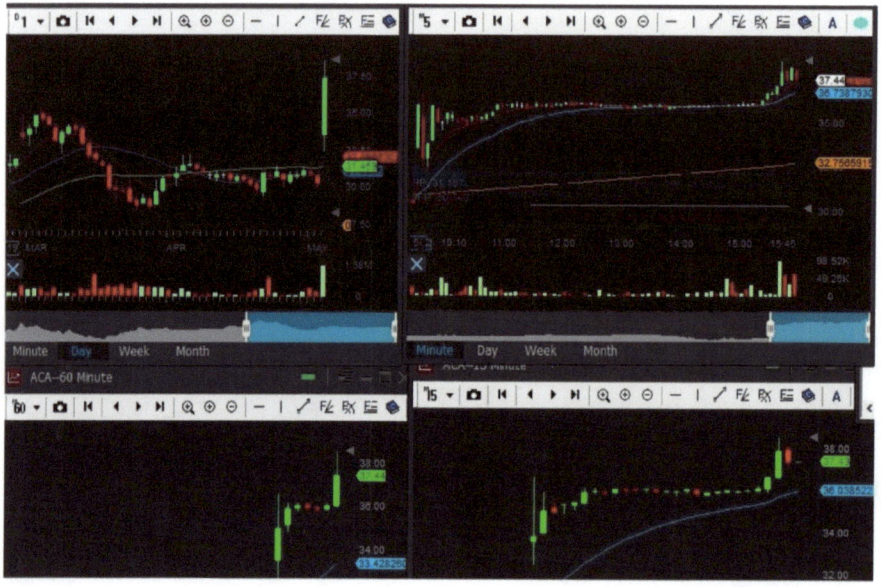

Example of a Break out followed by a Late day Break out

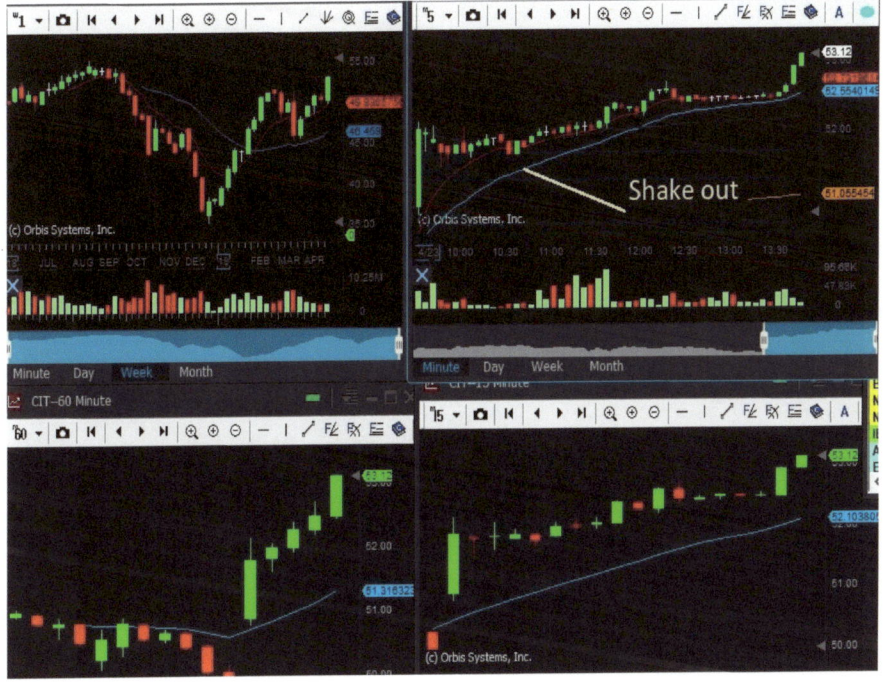

Shake out

Example of Late Day Break Down (this was the start of the move)

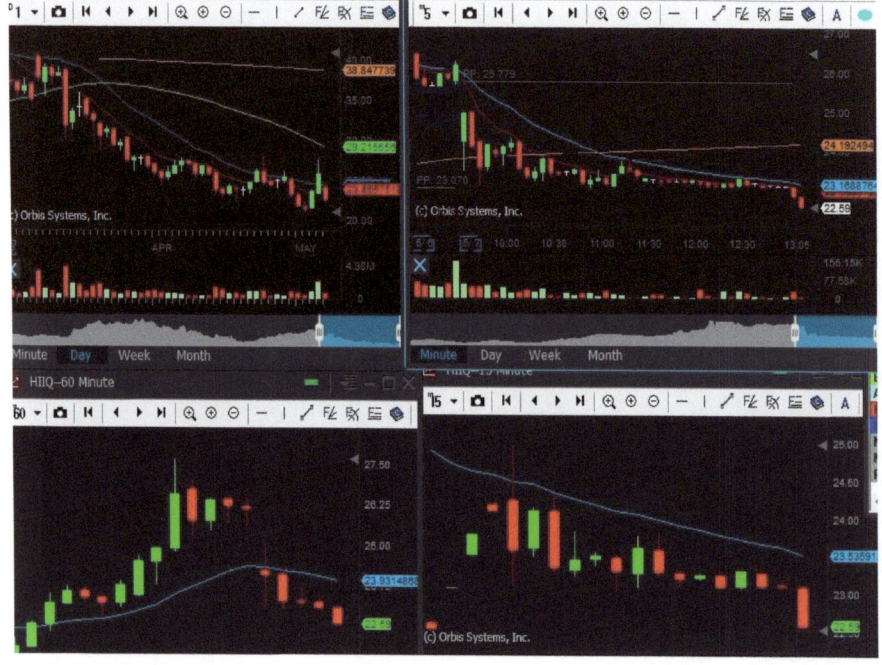

This type of trade strategy is covered in my book "3 Candle and 4 Candle Play"

Look at SWI; how many shares can you buy when you see tight consolidations and shakeouts in a row, that's an indication of adding more shares and tightening the stop loss to keep a fixed risk. Remember, never exit a trade as long as the stock moves in your favor. While trading charts like SWI, if a trader can't add more shares, they should at least keep the size they already have.

Free and easy scanning for the patterns

Scanning is the process of finding potential trade candidates. As we follow strict criteria for trading, it become very important that we use the right tools for scanning. As I always say '' speed and accuracy are the keys to successful trading business''. Let's discuss how I scan intraday charts:

1-   Trading platform

Almost all good trading platform provide options for selecting top gainers and losers (stocks). Link your charts to the top gainer and loser list and navigate the list quickly using up and down arrow if your platform allows, else click on each symbol to view same symbol on multiple time frame, as shown in the picture.

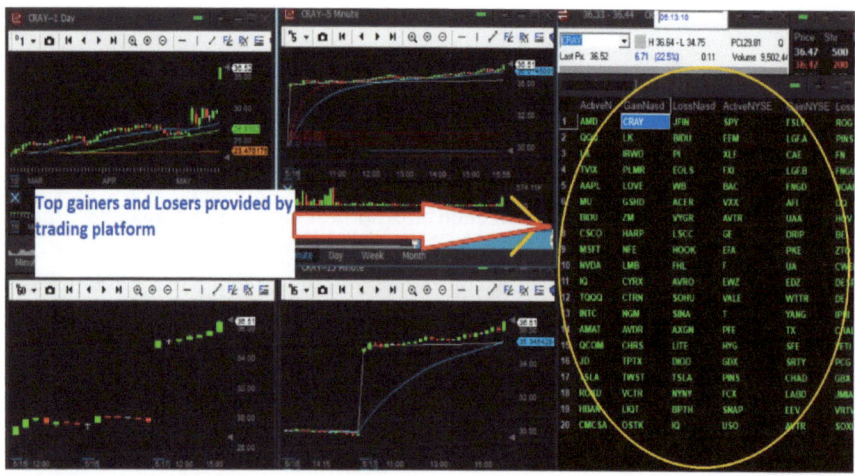

Once you find the charts meeting most of your criteria, you can save them to a watchlist and continue to monitor those symbols for trade entries.

2-   Use intraday scanners

If you have access to intraday scanners like trade-ideas etc to scan, that can be linked to your trading screens for daily gainers or loser, but I don't use that, these scanners affect the PC performance, slow the internet speed etc. I scan using a free web-based scanner, where I select my simple criteria and scroll the charts with a mouse, yes with a scroll of the mouse I glance the intraday and daily time frame. Many thanks to the developer of the website who made my life easy for free and no ads. Here is the link to that website: Click here

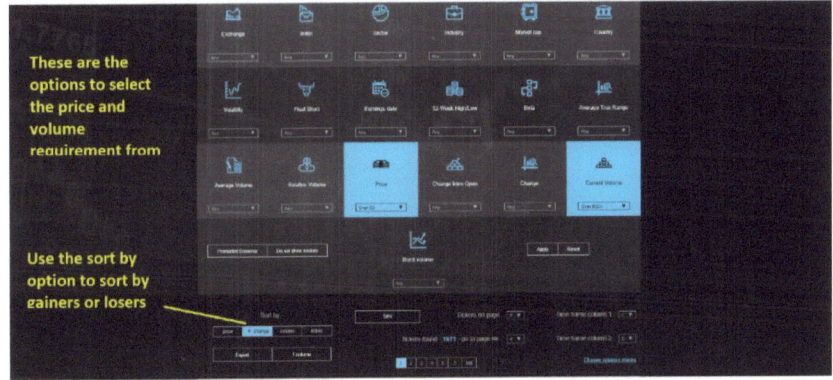

These are the options to select the price and volume requirement from

Use the sort by option to sort by gainers or losers

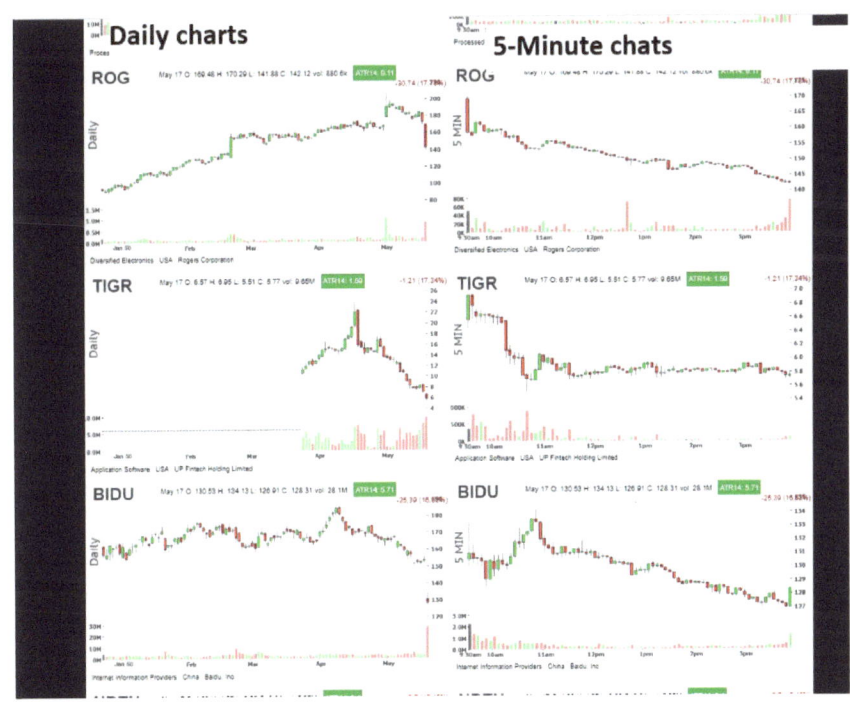

I am sure you would appreciate this scanner; the beauty is, these charts are easy to analyze on multiple time frames without the need to type symbols into your trading platform. Once you like a chart you add that symbol to your watchlist.

Other Paid Scanners:

Finviz, trade idea and TC200 are paid services which provide intraday real time charts.

Ending Notes

Congratulations! You have learnt advanced breakouts and breakdowns and I am really thankful you bought this book. You will appreciate the fact that this type of course is charged in 100s of dollars if not in thousands by the trading educators. I will submit that I did paid 1000s of dollars on training and mentoring when I started my trading career, but I wanted to help traders to get trading education for affordable price. So, I am trying to write individual strategies in book form and explaining each strategy in detail. All my strategy books have the same format where I explain trade criteria with examples, pattern requirements and provide trade management etc.

Once again, may I request yourself to leave a review to this book, your review will help other traders to get quality education on affordable price.

As always, please do not hesitate to reach me if you have any question on this strategy or you have other question. You can reach me via face book page **Profitable Trading Strategy, Book Series**, here is the link, (hey! do click the like button once you are there ☺)

https://www.facebook.com/ProfitableTradingStrategy.BookSeries/

Many thanks again, have a happy, healthy, wealthy and long life.

My Other Books
1- Trading Gaps for a Living- High Reward Gap Strategies
2- Profitable Trading Strategy- 3 Candle and 4 Candle Play

www.ingramcontent.com/pod-product-compliance
Lightning Source LLC
Chambersburg PA
CBHW041114180526
45172CB00001B/239